An Introductory Guide to Narcotics Anonymous

Revised

NARCOTICS ANONYMOUS
WORLD SERVICES, INC.
CHATSWORTH, CALIFORNIA

Copyright © 1991, 1992 by
Narcotics Anonymous World Services, Inc.
All rights reserved.
Published 1991. Enlarged 1992.
Printed in the United States of America.

World Service Office
PO Box 9999
Van Nuys, CA 91409 USA
Tel. (818) 773-9999 Fax (818) 700-0700
Website: www.na.org

World Service Office–CANADA
Mississauga, Ontario

World Service Office–EUROPE
Brussels, Belgium
T +32/2/646 6012

World Service Office–IRAN
Tehran, Iran
www.na-iran.org

Printed in China

This is NA Fellowship-approved literature.

Narcotics Anonymous, , ◇, ✦, and The NA Way
are registered trademarks of

Narcotics Anonymous World Services, Incorporated.

ISBN 978-1-55776-148-4   English   8/14
WSO Catalog Item No. EN-1200

The chapters in this book have been drawn from other material already published by Narcotics Anonymous World Services, Inc. They are reprinted here in their entirety. The items and respective copyright dates are as follows: The pamphlet *Am I an Addict?* (1983, 1988). *Welcome to Narcotics Anonymous* (1986, 1987). *For the Newcomer* (1983). *Another Look* (1976, 1984, 1992). "How It Works," Chapter Four of the book entitled *Narcotics Anonymous* (1982, 1983, 1984, 1986, 1987, 1988, 2008). *Self-Acceptance* (1985). *Sponsorship, Revised* (1983, 2004). *One Addict's Experience with Acceptance, Faith, and Commitment* (1983, 1992). *Just for Today* (1983). *Staying Clean on the Outside* (1987, 1988). *Recovery and Relapse*, published separately as a pamphlet (1976, 1986); its text is also included in its entirety in both the booklet (1976, 1983, 1986) and book (1982, 1983, 1984, 1986, 1987, 1988, 2008) entitled *Narcotics Anonymous*.

Table of Contents

Am I an Addict?

Only you can answer this question.

This may not be an easy thing to do. All through our usage, we told ourselves, "I can handle it." Even if this was true in the beginning, it is not so now. The drugs handled us. We lived to use and used to live. Very simply, an addict is a person whose life is controlled by drugs.

Perhaps you admit you have a problem with drugs, but you don't consider yourself an addict. All of us have preconceived ideas about what an addict is. There is nothing shameful about being an addict once you begin to take positive action. If you can identify with our problems, you may be able to identify with our solution. The following questions were written by recovering addicts in Narcotics Anonymous. If you have doubts about whether or not you're an addict, take a few moments to read the questions below and answer them as honestly as you can.

1. Do you ever use alone?

    Yes ☐   No ☐

2. Have you ever substituted one drug for another, thinking that one particular drug was the problem?

    Yes ☐   No ☐

3. Have you ever manipulated or lied to a doctor to obtain prescription drugs?   Yes ☐   No ☐

4. Have you ever stolen drugs or stolen to obtain drugs?   Yes ☐   No ☐

5. Do you regularly use a drug when you wake up or when you go to bed?   Yes ☐   No ☐

6. Have you ever taken one drug to overcome the effects of another?

    Yes ☐   No ☐

7. Do you avoid people or places that do not approve of you using drugs?

    Yes ☐   No ☐

8. Have you ever used a drug without knowing what it was or what it would do to you? Yes ☐ No ☐

9. Has your job or school performance ever suffered from the effects of your drug use? Yes ☐ No ☐

10. Have you ever been arrested as a result of using drugs? Yes ☐ No ☐

11. Have you ever lied about what or how much you use? Yes ☐ No ☐

12. Do you put the purchase of drugs ahead of your financial responsibilities? Yes ☐ No ☐

13. Have you ever tried to stop or control your using? Yes ☐ No ☐

14. Have you ever been in a jail, hospital, or drug rehabilitation center because of your using? Yes ☐ No ☐

15. Does using interfere with your sleeping or eating? Yes ☐ No ☐

16. Does the thought of running out of drugs terrify you? Yes ☐ No ☐

17. Do you feel it is impossible for you to live without drugs? Yes ☐ No ☐

18. Do you ever question your own sanity? Yes ☐ No ☐

19. Is your drug use making life at home unhappy? Yes ☐ No ☐

20. Have you ever thought you couldn't fit in or have a good time without drugs? Yes ☐ No ☐

21. Have you ever felt defensive, guilty, or ashamed about your using? Yes ☐ No ☐

22. Do you think a lot about drugs? Yes ☐ No ☐

23. Have you had irrational or indefinable fears? Yes ☐ No ☐

24. Has using affected your sexual relationships? Yes ☐ No ☐

25. Have you ever taken drugs you didn't prefer? Yes ☐ No ☐

26. Have you ever used drugs because of emotional pain or stress? Yes ☐ No ☐

27. Have you ever overdosed on any drugs?   Yes ☐   No ☐

28. Do you continue to use despite negative consequences?

                              Yes ☐   No ☐

29. Do you think you might have a drug problem?   Yes ☐   No ☐

"Am I an addict?" This is a question only you can answer. We found that we all answered different numbers of these questions "Yes." The actual number of "Yes" responses wasn't as important as how we felt inside and how addiction had affected our lives.

Some of these questions don't even mention drugs. This is because addiction is an insidious disease that affects all areas of our lives—even those areas which seem at first to have little to do with drugs. The different drugs we used were not as important as why we used them and what they did to us.

When we first read these questions, it was frightening for us to think we might be addicts. Some of us tried to dismiss these thoughts by saying:

"Oh, those questions don't make sense;"

Or,

"I'm different. I know I take drugs, but I'm not an addict. I have real emotional/family/job problems;"

Or,

"I'm just having a tough time getting it together right now;"

Or,

"I'll be able to stop when I find the right person/get the right job, etc."

If you are an addict, you must first admit that you have a problem with drugs before any progress can be made toward recovery. These questions, when honestly approached, may help to show you how using drugs has made your life unmanageable. Addiction is a disease which, without recovery, ends in jails, institutions, and death. Many of us came to Narcotics Anonymous because drugs had stopped doing what we needed them to do. Addiction takes our pride, self-esteem, family, loved ones, and even our desire to live. If you have not reached this point in your addiction, you don't have to. We have found that our own private hell was within us. If you want help, you can find it in the Fellowship of Narcotics Anonymous.

"We were searching for an answer when we reached out and found Narcotics Anonymous. We came to our first NA meeting in defeat and didn't know what to expect. After sitting in a meeting, or several meetings, we began to feel that people cared and were willing to help. Although our minds told us that we would never make it, the people in the fellowship gave us hope by insisting that we could recover. […] Surrounded by fellow addicts, we realized that we were not alone anymore. Recovery is what happens in our meetings. Our lives are at stake. We found that by putting recovery first, the program works. We faced three disturbing realizations:

1. We are powerless over addiction and our lives are unmanageable;

2. Although we are not responsible for our disease, we are responsible for our recovery;

3. We can no longer blame people, places, and things for our addiction. We must face our problems and our feelings.

The ultimate weapon for recovery is the recovering addict." [1]

---

[1] Basic Text, *Narcotics Anonymous*

Welcome to
Narcotics Anonymous

This pamphlet was written to answer some of your questions concerning the program of Narcotics Anonymous. Our message is very simple: We have found a way to live without using drugs, and we are happy to share it with anyone for whom drugs are a problem.

Welcome to your first NA meeting. NA offers addicts a way to live drug-free. If you are not sure you're an addict, don't worry about it; just keep coming to our meetings. You will have all the time you need to make up your own mind.

If you are like many of us when we attended our first NA meeting, you may be feeling pretty nervous and think that everyone at the meeting is focusing on you. If so, you are not the only one. Many of us have felt the same way. It has been said, "If your stomach's all tied up in knots, you're probably in the right place." We often say that no one comes through the doors of NA by mistake. Nonaddicted people don't spend their time wondering if they're addicts. They don't even think about it. If you're wondering whether or not you're an addict, you might be one. Just allow yourself the time to listen to us share about what it has been like for us. Perhaps you will hear something that sounds familiar to you. It doesn't matter whether or not you have used the same drugs others mention. It is not important which drugs you used; you're welcome here if you want to stop using. Most addicts experience very similar feelings, and it is in focusing on our similarities, rather than our differences, that we are helpful to one another.

You may be feeling hopeless and afraid. You may think that this program, like other things you have tried, will not work. Or you may think that it will work for someone else but not for you because you feel you are different than us. Most of us felt like that when we first came to NA. Somehow we knew that we couldn't go on using drugs, but we didn't know how to stop or stay clean. We were all afraid to let go of something that had become so important to us. It is a relief to discover that the only requirement for membership in NA is a *desire* to stop using.

At first, most of us were mistrustful and fearful of trying a new way of doing things. About the only thing we were sure of was that our old ways were not working at all. Even after getting clean, things didn't change right away. Often, even our usual activities, such as driving a car or using the telephone, seemed frightening and strange, as if we had become someone we didn't recognize. This is where the fellowship and support of other clean addicts really helps, and we begin to rely on others for the reassurance we so desperately need.

You may already be thinking: "Yes, but" or "What if?" However, even if you have doubts, you can use these simple suggestions for starters: Attend as many NA meetings as you can and collect a list of NA phone numbers to use regularly, especially when the urge for drugs is strong. The temptation is not restricted to the days and hours where meetings occur. We are clean today because we reached out for help. What helped us can help you. So don't be afraid to call another recovering addict.

The only way to keep from returning to active addiction is not to take that first drug. The most natural thing for an addict to do is to use drugs. In order for most of us to abstain from using mood-altering, mind-changing chemicals, we have had to undergo drastic changes physically, mentally, emotionally, and spiritually. The Twelve Steps of NA offer us a way to change. As someone said: "You can probably get clean by just coming to meetings. However, if you want to stay clean and experience recovery, you will need to practice the Twelve Steps." This is more than we can do alone. In the NA Fellowship, we support one another in our efforts to learn and practice a new way of living that keeps us healthy and drug-free.

At your first meeting, you will meet people with various lengths of clean time. You may wonder how they could remain clean for that period of time. If you keep coming to NA meetings and stay clean, you will come to understand how it works. There is a mutual respect and caring among clean addicts because we've all had to overcome the misery of addiction. We love and support each other in our recovery. The program of NA is comprised of spiritual principles that we have found help us to remain clean. Nothing will be demanded of you, but you will receive many suggestions. This fellowship provides the opportunity for us to give you what we have found: a clean way of living. We know that we have to "give it away in order to keep it."

So, welcome! We are glad that you have made it here, and hope that you decide to stay. It is important for you to know that you will hear God mentioned at NA meetings. What we are referring to is a Power greater than ourselves that makes possible what seems impossible. We found that Power here, in NA, in the program, in the meetings, and in the people. This is the spiritual principle that has worked for us to live drug-free a day at a time; and whenever a day is too long, then five minutes at a time. We can do together what we could not do alone. We invite you to use our strength and our hope until you have found some of your own. There will come a time when you too may want to share with someone else what has been freely given to you.

KEEP COMING BACK—IT WORKS!

For the Newcomer

NA is a nonprofit fellowship or society of men and women for whom drugs had become a major problem. We are recovering addicts who meet regularly to help each other to stay clean. There are no dues or fees. The only requirement for membership is the desire to stop using.

You don't have to be clean when you get here, but after your first meeting we suggest that you keep coming back and come clean. You don't have to wait for an overdose or jail sentence to get help from NA, nor is addiction a hopeless condition from which there is no recovery. It is possible to overcome the desire to use drugs with the help of the Twelve Step program of Narcotics Anonymous and the fellowship of recovering addicts.

Addiction is a disease that can happen to anyone. Some of us used drugs because we enjoyed them, while others used to suppress the feelings we already had. Still others suffered from physical or mental ailments and became addicted to the medication prescribed during our illnesses. Some of us joined the crowd using drugs a few times just to be cool and later found that we could not stop.

Many of us tried to overcome addiction, and sometimes temporary relief was possible, but it was usually followed by an even deeper involvement than before.

Whatever the circumstances, it really doesn't matter. Addiction is a progressive disease such as diabetes. We are allergic to drugs. Our ends are always the same: jails, institutions, or death. If life has become unmanageable and you want to live without it being necessary to use drugs, we have found a way. Here are the Twelve Steps of Narcotics Anonymous that we use on a daily basis to help us overcome our disease.

1. We admitted that we were powerless over our addiction, that our lives had become unmanageable.

2. We came to believe that a Power greater than ourselves could restore us to sanity.

3. We made a decision to turn our will and our lives over to the care of God *as we understood Him.*

4. We made a searching and fearless moral inventory of ourselves.

5. We admitted to God, to ourselves, and to another human being the exact nature of our wrongs.

6. We were entirely ready to have God remove all these defects of character.

7. We humbly asked Him to remove our shortcomings.

8. We made a list of all persons we had harmed, and became willing to make amends to them all.

9. We made direct amends to such people wherever possible, except when to do so would injure them or others.

10. We continued to take personal inventory and when we were wrong promptly admitted it.

11. We sought through prayer and meditation to improve our conscious contact with God *as we understood Him*, praying only for knowledge of His will for us and the power to carry that out.

12. Having had a spiritual awakening as a result of these steps, we tried to carry this message to addicts, and to practice these principles in all our affairs.

Recovery doesn't stop with just being clean. As we abstain from all drugs (and, yes this means alcohol and marijuana, too) we come face-to-face with feelings that we have never coped with successfully. We even experience feelings we were not capable of having in the past. We must become willing to meet old and new feelings as they come.

We learn to experience feelings and realize they can do us no harm unless we act on them. Rather than acting on them, we call an NA member if we have feelings we cannot handle. By sharing, we learn to work through it. Chances are they've had a similar experience and can relate what worked for them. Remember, an addict alone is in bad company.

The Twelve Steps, new friends, and sponsors all help us deal with these feelings. In NA, our joys are multiplied by sharing good days; our sorrows are lessened by sharing the bad. For the first time in our lives, we don't have to experience anything alone. Now that we have a group, we are able to develop a relationship with a Higher Power that can always be with us.

We suggest that you look for a sponsor as soon as you become acquainted with the members in your area. Being asked to sponsor a new member is a privilege so don't hesitate to ask someone. Sponsorship is a rewarding experience for both; we are all here to help and be helped. We who are recovering must share with you what we have learned in order to maintain our growth in the NA program and our ability to function without drugs.

This program offers hope. All you have to bring with you is the desire to stop using and the willingness to try this new way of life.

Come to meetings, listen with an open mind, ask questions, get phone numbers and use them. Stay clean just for today.

May we also remind you that this is an *anonymous* program and your anonymity will be held in the strictest of confidence. "We are not interested in what or how much you used or who your connections were, what you have done in the past, how much or how little you have, but only in what you want to do about your problem and how we can help."

Another Look

There are probably as many definitions of addiction as there are ways of thinking, based on both research and personal experience. It is not surprising that there are many areas of honest disagreement in the definitions that we hear. Some seem to fit the observed and known facts for some groups better than for others. If we can accept this as a fact, then perhaps another viewpoint ought to be examined, in the hope that we can discover a way more basic to all addictions and more valid in establishing communication among all of us. If we can find greater agreement on *what addiction is not,* then perhaps *what it is* may appear with greater clarity.

Maybe we can agree on some prime points.

1. Addiction is not freedom.

The very nature of our disease and its observed symptoms point up this fact. We addicts value personal freedom highly, perhaps because we want it so much and experience it so seldom in the progression of our illness. Even in periods of abstinence, freedom is curtailed. We are never quite sure if any action is based in a conscious desire for continued recovery or an unconscious wish to return to using. We seek to manipulate people and conditions and control all our actions; thus we destroy spontaneity, an integral mark of freedom. We fail to realize that the need for control springs from a fear of losing control. This fear, based in part on past failures and disappointments in solving life's difficulties, prevents us from making meaningful choices; choices which, if acted upon, would remove the very fear which blocks us.

2. Addiction is not personal growth.

The monotonous, imitative, ritualistic, compulsive, and obsessive routines of active addiction render us incapable of responsive or meaningful thought and action. Personal growth is creative effort and purposeful behavior; it presupposes choice, change, and the capacity to face life on its own terms.

3. Addiction is not goodwill.

Addiction insulates us from people, places, and things outside of our own world of getting, using, and finding ways and means to continue the process. Hostile, resentful, self-centered, and self-concerned, we cut off all outside interests as our illness progresses. We live in fear and suspicion of the very people we have to depend on for our needs. This touches every area of our lives and anything not completely familiar becomes alien and dangerous. Our world shrinks and isolation is its goal. This might well be the true nature of our disorder.

All that has been said above could be summed up in…

4. Addiction is not a way of life.

The sick, self-seeking, self-centered, and self-enclosed world of the addict hardly qualifies as a way of life; at best, perhaps it is a way to survive for awhile. Even in this limited existence it is a way of despair, destruction, and death.

Any lifestyle seeking spiritual fulfillment seems to demand the very things missing in addiction: *freedom, goodwill, creative action,* and *personal growth.*

With freedom, life is a meaningful, changing, and advancing process. It looks forward with a reasonable expectancy to a better and richer realization of our desires and a greater fulfillment of our personal selves. These are, of course, some of the manifestations of the spiritual progress that results from the daily practice of the Twelve Steps of NA.

Goodwill is an action that includes others besides ourselves—a way that considers others as important in their own lives as we are in ours. It is hard to tell whether goodwill is the key to empathy or vice versa. If we accept empathy as the capacity to see ourselves in others knowingly, without losing our own identity, then we recognize a sameness in both. If we have accepted ourselves, how can we reject another? Affection comes from seeing similarities. Intolerance results from differences we will not accept.

In personal growth, we use both freedom and goodwill in cooperation with others. We realize we cannot live alone, that personal growth is also interpersonal growth. In order to find better balance, we examine personal, social, and spiritual values as well as material values. Maturity seems to demand this kind of evaluation.

In active addiction, insanity, institutions, and death are the only ends. In recovery, through the help of a Higher Power and the steps of NA, anything is possible.

Creative action is not a mysterious procedure, although it is an inside job in rebuilding or reintegrating our disordered and fractured personalities. Often, it means simply listening to those hunches and intuitive feelings that we think would benefit others or ourselves, and acting on them spontaneously. Here is where many basic principles of action become apparent. We are then able to make decisions based on principles that have real value to ourselves.

The purpose of the Twelve Steps of Narcotics Anonymous becomes clear as we find that dependence on a Higher Power, as we each understand It, brings self-respect and self-reliance. We know that we are neither superior nor inferior to anyone; our real value lies in being ourselves. Freedom, with responsibility for ourselves and our actions, appears to be foremost in our lives. We keep and expand freedom through daily practice; this is the creative action that never ends. Goodwill, of course, is the beginning of all spiritual growth. It leads to affection and love in all our actions. These three goals, *freedom, creative action,* and *goodwill* when shown in service in the fellowship, without seeking personal rewards, bring about changes whose ends we cannot predict or control. Therefore, service is also a Power greater than we, and has significant meaning for all.

**My gratitude speaks
when I care and
when I share
with others the NA way**

How It Works

If you want what we have to offer, and are willing to make the effort to get it, then you are ready to take certain steps. These are the principles that made our recovery possible.

1. *We admitted that we were powerless over our addiction, that our lives had become unmanageable.*

2. *We came to believe that a Power greater than ourselves could restore us to sanity.*

3. *We made a decision to turn our will and our lives over to the care of God as we understood Him.*

4. *We made a searching and fearless moral inventory of ourselves.*

5. *We admitted to God, to ourselves, and to another human being the exact nature of our wrongs.*

6. *We were entirely ready to have God remove all these defects of character.*

7. *We humbly asked Him to remove our shortcomings.*

8. *We made a list of all persons we had harmed, and became willing to make amends to them all.*

9. *We made direct amends to such people wherever possible, except when to do so would injure them or others.*

10. *We continued to take personal inventory and when we were wrong promptly admitted it.*

11. *We sought through prayer and meditation to improve our conscious contact with* God *as we understood Him,* praying only for knowledge of His will for us and the power to carry that out.

12. *Having had a spiritual awakening as a result of these steps, we tried to carry this message to addicts, and to practice these principles in all our affairs.*

This sounds like a big order, and we can't do it all at once. We didn't become addicted in one day, so remember—easy does it.

There is one thing more than anything else that will defeat us in our recovery; this is an attitude of indifference or intolerance toward spiritual principles. Three of these that are indispensable are honesty, open-mindedness, and willingness. With these we are well on our way.

We feel that our approach to the disease of addiction is completely realistic for the thera-peutic value of one addict helping another is without parallel. We feel that our way is prac-tical, for one addict can best understand and help another addict. We believe that the sooner we face our problems within our society, in everyday living, just that much faster do we become acceptable, responsible, and productive members of that society.

The only way to keep from returning to ac-tive addiction is not to take that first drug. If you are like us you know that one is too many and a thousand never enough. We put great emphasis on this, for we know that when we use drugs in any form, or substitute one for an-other, we release our addiction all over again.

Thinking of alcohol as different from other drugs has caused a great many addicts to relapse. Before we came to NA, many of us viewed alcohol separately, but we cannot afford to be confused about this. Alcohol is a drug. We are people with the disease of addiction who must abstain from all drugs in order to recover.

These are some of the questions we have asked ourselves: Are we sure we want to stop using? Do we understand that we have no real control over drugs? Do we recognize that, in the long run, we didn't use drugs—they used us? Did jails and institutions take over the management of our lives at different times? Do we fully accept the fact that our every attempt to stop using or to control our using failed? Do we know that our addiction changed us into someone we didn't want to be: dishonest, deceitful, self-willed people at odds with ourselves and our fellow man? Do we really believe that we have failed as drug users?

When we were using, reality became so painful that oblivion was preferable. We tried to keep other people from knowing about our pain. We isolated ourselves, and lived in prisons that we built with loneliness. Through this desperation, we sought help in Narcotics Anonymous. When we come to NA we are physically, mentally, and spiritually bankrupt. We have hurt so long that we are willing to go to any length to stay clean.

Our only hope is to live by the example of those who have faced our dilemma and have found a way out. Regardless of who we are, where we came from, or what we have done, we are accepted in NA. Our addiction gives us a common ground for understanding one another.

As a result of attending a few meetings, we begin to feel like we finally belong somewhere. It is in these meetings that we are introduced to the Twelve Steps of Narcotics Anonymous. We learn to work the steps in the order that they are written and to use them on a daily basis. The steps are our solution. They are our survival kit. They are our defense against addiction, which is a deadly disease. Our steps are the principles that make our recovery possible.

Step One

"We admitted that we were powerless over our addiction, that our lives had become unmanageable."

It doesn't matter what or how much we used. In Narcotics Anonymous, staying clean has to come first. We realize that we cannot use drugs and live. When we admit our powerlessness and our inability to manage our own lives, we open the door to recovery. No one could convince us that we were addicts. It is an admission that we have to make for ourselves. When some of us have doubts, we ask ourselves this question: "Can I control my use of any form of mind or mood-altering chemicals?"

Most addicts will see that control is impossible the moment it is suggested. Whatever the outcome, we find that we cannot control our using for any length of time.

This would clearly suggest that an addict has no control over drugs. Powerlessness means using drugs against our will. If we can't stop using, how can we tell ourselves we are in control? The inability to stop using, even with the greatest willpower and the most sincere desire, is what we mean when we say, "We have absolutely no choice." However, we do have a choice after we stop trying to justify our using.

We didn't stumble into this fellowship brimming with love, honesty, openmindedness, or willingness. We reached a point where we could no longer continue using because of physical, mental, and spiritual pain. When we were beaten, we became willing.

Our inability to control our usage of drugs is a symptom of the disease of addiction. We are powerless not only over drugs, but over our addiction as well. We need to admit this fact in order to recover. Addiction is a physical, mental, and spiritual disease that affects every area of our lives.

The physical aspect of our disease is the compulsive use of drugs: the inability to stop using once we have started. The mental aspect of our disease is the obsession, or overpowering desire to use, even when we are destroying our lives. The spiritual part of our disease is our total self-centeredness. We felt that we could stop whenever we wanted to, despite all evidence to the contrary. Denial, substitution, rationalization, justification, distrust of others, guilt, embarrassment, dereliction, degradation, isolation, and loss of control are all results of our disease. Our disease is progressive, incurable, and fatal. Most of us are relieved to find out we have a disease instead of a moral deficiency.

We are not responsible for our disease, but we are responsible for our recovery.

Most of us tried to stop using on our own, but we were unable to live with or without drugs. Eventually, we realized that we were powerless over our addiction.

Many of us tried to stop using on sheer willpower. This action was a temporary solution. We saw that willpower alone would not work for any length of time. We tried countless other remedies—psychiatrists, hospitals, recovery houses, lovers, new towns, new jobs. Everything that we tried, failed. We began to see that we had rationalized the most outrageous sort of nonsense to justify the mess that we made of our lives with drugs.

Until we let go of our reservations, no matter what they are, the foundation of our recovery is in danger. Reservations rob us of the benefits that this program has to offer. In ridding ourselves of all reservations, we surrender. Then, and only then, can we be helped to recover from the disease of addiction.

Now, the question is: "If we are powerless, how can Narcotics Anonymous help?" We begin by asking for help. The foundation of our program is the admission that we, of ourselves, do not have power over addiction. When we can accept this fact, we have completed the first part of Step One.

A second admission must be made before our foundation is complete. If we stop here, we will know only half the truth. We are great ones for manipulating the truth. We say on one hand, "Yes, I am powerless over my addiction," and on the other hand, "When I get my life together, I can handle drugs." Such thoughts and actions led us back to active addiction. It never occurred to us to ask, "If we can't control our addiction, how can we control our lives?" We felt miserable without drugs, and our lives were unmanageable.

Unemployability, dereliction, and destruction are easily seen as characteristics of an unmanageable life. Our families generally are disappointed, baffled, and confused by our actions and often desert or disown us. Becoming employed, socially acceptable, and reunited with our families does not make our lives manageable. Social acceptability does not equal recovery.

We have found that we had no choice except to completely change our old ways of thinking or go back to using. When we give our best, it works for us as it has worked for others. When we could no longer stand our old ways, we began to change. From that point forward, we began to see that every clean day is a successful day, no matter what happens. Surrender means not having to fight anymore. We accept our addiction and life the way it is. We become willing to do whatever is necessary to stay clean, even the things we don't like doing.

Until we took Step One, we were full of fear and doubt. At this point, many of us felt lost and confused. We felt different. Upon working this step, we affirmed our surrender to the principles of NA. Only after surrender are we able to overcome the alienation of addiction. Help for addicts begins only when we are able to admit complete defeat. This can be frightening, but it is the foundation on which we built our lives.

Step One means that we do not have to use, and this is a great freedom. It took a while for some of us to realize that our lives had become unmanageable. For others, the unmanageability of their lives was the only thing that was clear. We knew in our hearts that drugs had the power to change us into someone that we didn't want to be.

Being clean and working this step, we are released from our chains. However, none of the steps work by magic. We do not just say the words of this step; we learn to live them. We see for ourselves that the program has something to offer us.

We have found hope. We can learn to function in the world in which we live. We can find meaning and purpose in life and be rescued from insanity, depravity, and death.

When we admit our powerlessness and inability to manage our own lives, we open the door for a Power greater than ourselves to help us. It is not where we were that counts, but where we are going.

Step Two

"We came to believe that a Power greater than ourselves could restore us to sanity."

The Second Step is necessary if we expect to achieve ongoing recovery. The First Step leaves us with a need to believe in something that can help us with our powerlessness, uselessness, and helplessness.

The First Step has left a vacuum in our lives. We need to find something to fill that void. This is the purpose of the Second Step.

Some of us didn't take this step seriously at first; we passed over it with a minimum of concern, only to find the next steps would not work until we worked Step Two. Even when we admitted that we needed help with our drug problem, many of us would not admit to the need for faith and sanity.

We have a disease: progressive, incurable, and fatal. One way or another we went out and bought our destruction on the time payment plan! All of us, from the junkie snatching purses to the sweet little old lady hitting two or three doctors for legal prescriptions, have one thing in common: we seek our destruction a bag at a time, a few pills at a time, or a bottle at a time until we die. This is at least part of the insanity of addiction. The price may seem higher for the addict who prostitutes for a fix than it is for the addict who merely lies to a doctor. Ultimately, both pay for their disease with their lives. Insanity is repeating the same mistakes and expecting different results.

Many of us realize when we get to the program that we have gone back time and again to using, even though we knew that we were destroying our lives. Insanity is using drugs, day after day, knowing that only physical and mental destruction comes when we use. The most obvious insanity of the disease of addiction is the obsession to use drugs.

Ask yourself this question, Do I believe it would be insane to walk up to someone and say, "May I please have a heart attack or a fatal accident?" If you can agree that this would be an insane thing, you should have no problem with the Second Step.

In this program, the first thing we do is stop using drugs. At this point, we begin to feel the pain of living without drugs or anything to replace them. The pain forces us to seek a Power greater than ourselves that can relieve our obsession to use.

The process of coming to believe is similar for most addicts. Most of us lacked a working relationship with a Higher Power. We begin to develop this relationship by simply admitting to the possibility of a Power greater than ourselves. Most of us have no trouble admitting that addiction had become a destructive force in our lives. Our best efforts resulted in ever greater destruction and despair. At some point, we realized that we needed the help of some Power greater than our addiction. Our understanding of a Higher Power is up to us. No one is going to decide for us. We can call it the group, the program, or we can call it God. The only suggested guidelines are that this Power be loving, caring, and greater than ourselves. We don't have to be religious to accept this idea. The point is that we open our minds to believe. We may have difficulty with this, but by keeping an open mind, sooner or later, we find the help we need.

We talked and listened to others. We saw other people recovering, and they told us what was working for them. We began to see evidence of some Power that could not be fully explained. Confronted with this evidence, we began to accept the existence of a Power greater than ourselves. We can use this Power long before we understand it.

As we see coincidences and miracles happening in our lives, acceptance becomes trust. We grow to feel comfortable with our Higher Power as a source of strength. As we learn to trust this Power, we begin to overcome our fear of life.

The process of coming to believe restores us to sanity. The strength to move into action comes from this belief. We need to accept this step to start on the road to recovery. When our belief has grown, we are ready for Step Three.

Step Three

"We made a decision to turn our will and our lives over to the care of God as we understood Him.*"*

As addicts, we turned our will and our lives over many times to a destructive power. Our will and our lives were controlled by drugs. We were trapped by our need for instant gratification that drugs gave us. During that time, our total being—body, mind, and spirit—was dominated by drugs. For a time, it was pleasurable, then the euphoria began to wear off and we saw the ugly side of addiction. We found that the higher our drugs took us, the lower they brought us. We faced two choices: either we suffered the pain of withdrawal or took more drugs.

For all of us, the day came when there was no longer a choice; we had to use. Having given our will and lives to our addiction, in utter desperation, we looked for another way. In Narcotics Anonymous, we decide to turn our will and our lives over to the care of God as we understand Him. This is a giant step. We don't have to be religious; anyone can take this step. All that is required is willingness. All that is essential is that we open the door to a Power greater than ourselves.

Our concept of God comes not from dogma but from what we believe and from what works for us. Many of us understand God to be simply whatever force keeps us clean. The right to a God of your understanding is total and without any catches. Because we have this right, it is necessary to be honest about our belief if we are to grow spiritually.

We found that all we needed to do was try. When we gave our best effort, the program worked for us as it has worked for countless others. The Third Step does not say, "We turned our will and our lives over to the care of God." It says, *"We made a decision to turn our will and our lives over to the care of God* as we understood Him." We made the decision; it was not made for us by the drugs, our families, a probation officer, judge, therapist, or doctor. We made it! For the first time since that first high, we have made a decision for ourselves.

The word decision implies action. This decision is based on faith. We have only to believe that the miracle that we see working in the lives of clean addicts can happen to any addict with the desire to change. We simply realize there is a force for spiritual growth that can help us become more tolerant, patient, and useful in helping others. Many of us have said, "Take my will and my life. Guide me in my recovery. Show me how to live." The relief of "letting go and letting God" helps us develop a life that is worth living.

Surrendering to the will of our Higher Power gets easier with daily practice. When we honestly try, it works. Many of us start our day with a simple request for guidance from our Higher Power.

Although we know that "turning it over" works, we may still take our will and life back. We may even get angry because God permits it. At times during our recovery, the decision to ask for God's help is our greatest source of strength and courage. We cannot make this decision often enough. We surrender quietly, and let the God of our understanding take care of us.

At first, our heads reeled with the questions: "What will happen when I turn my life over? Will I become 'perfect'?" We may have been more realistic than this. Some of us had to turn to an experienced NA member and ask, "What was it like for you?" The answer will vary from member to member. Most of us feel open-mindedness, willingness, and surrender are the keys to this step.

We have surrendered our will and our lives to the care of a Power greater than ourselves. If we are thorough and sincere, we will notice a change for the better. Our fears are lessened, and faith begins to grow as we learn the true meaning of surrender. We are no longer fighting fear, anger, guilt, self-pity, or depression. We realize that the Power that brought us to this program is still with us and will continue to guide us if we allow It. We are slowly beginning to lose the paralyzing fear of hopelessness. The proof of this step is shown in the way we live.

We have come to enjoy living clean and want more of the good things that the NA Fellowship holds for us. We know now that we cannot pause in our spiritual program; we want all that we can get.

We are now ready for our first honest self-appraisal, and we begin with Step Four.

Step Four

"We made a searching and fearless moral inventory of ourselves."

The purpose of a searching and fearless moral inventory is to sort through the confusion and the contradiction of our lives, so that we can find out who we really are. We are starting a new way of life and need to be rid of the burdens and traps that controlled us and prevented our growth.

As we approach this step, most of us are afraid that there is a monster inside of us that, if released, will destroy us. This fear can cause us to put off our inventory or may even prevent us from taking this crucial step at all. We have found that fear is a lack of faith, and we have found a loving, personal God to whom we can turn. We no longer need to be afraid.

We have been experts at self-deception and rationalization. By writing our inventory, we can overcome these obstacles. A written inventory will unlock parts of our subconscious that remain hidden when we simply think about or talk about who we are. Once it is all down on paper, it is much easier to see, and much harder to deny our true nature. Honest self-assessment is one of the keys to our new way of life.

Let's face it; when we were using, we were not honest with ourselves. We are becoming honest with ourselves when we admit that addiction has defeated us and that we need help. It took a long time to admit that we were beaten. We found that we do not recover physically, mentally, or spiritually overnight. Step Four will help us toward our recovery. Most of us find that we were neither as terrible, nor as wonderful, as we supposed. We are surprised to find that we have good points in our inventory. Anyone who has some time in the program and has worked this step will tell you that the Fourth Step was a turning point in their life.

Some of us make the mistake of approaching the Fourth Step as if it were a confession of how horrible we are—what a bad person we have been. In this new way of life, a binge of emotional sorrow can be dangerous. This is not the purpose of the Fourth Step. We are trying to free ourselves of living in old, useless patterns. We take the Fourth Step to grow and to gain strength and insight. We may approach the Fourth Step in a number of ways.

To have the faith and courage to write a fearless inventory, Steps One, Two, and Three are the necessary preparation. It is advisable that before we start, we go over the first three steps with a sponsor. We get comfortable with our understanding of these steps. We allow ourselves the privilege of feeling good about what we are doing. We have been thrashing about for a long time and have gotten nowhere. Now we start the Fourth Step and let go of fear. We simply put it on paper, to the best of our present ability.

We must be done with the past, not cling to it. We want to look our past in the face, see it for what it really was, and release it so we can live today. The past, for most of us, has been a ghost in the closet. We have been afraid to open that closet for fear of what that ghost may do to us. We do not have to look at the past alone. Our wills and our lives are now in the hands of our Higher Power.

Writing a thorough and honest inventory seemed impossible. It was, as long as we were operating under our own power. We take a few quiet moments before writing and ask for the strength to be fearless and thorough.

In Step Four, we begin to get in touch with ourselves. We write about our liabilities such as guilt, shame, remorse, self-pity, resentment, anger, depression, frustration, confusion, loneliness, anxiety, betrayal, hopelessness, failure, fear, and denial.

We write about the things that bother us here and now. We have a tendency to think negatively, so putting it on paper gives us a chance to look more positively at what is happening.

Assets must also be considered, if we are to get an accurate and complete picture of ourselves. This is very difficult for most of us, because it is hard to accept that we have good qualities. However, we all have assets, many of them newly found in the program, such as being clean, open-mindedness, God-awareness, honesty with others, acceptance, positive action, sharing, willingness, courage, faith, caring, gratitude, kindness, and generosity. Also, our inventories usually include material on relationships.

We review our past performance and our present behavior to see what we want to keep and what we want to discard. No one is forcing us to give up our misery. This step has the reputation of being difficult; in reality, it is quite simple.

We write our inventory without considering the Fifth Step. We work Step Four as if there were no Step Five. We can write alone or near other people; whatever is more comfortable to the writer is fine. We can write as long or as short as needed.

Someone with experience can help. The important thing is to write a moral inventory. If the word moral bothers us, we may call it a positive/negative inventory.

The way to write an inventory is to write it! Thinking about an inventory, talking about it, theorizing about the inventory will not get it written. We sit down with a notebook, ask for guidance, pick up our pen and start writing. Anything we think about is inventory material. When we realize how little we have to lose, and how much we have to gain, we begin this step.

A basic rule of thumb is that we can write too little, yet we can never write too much. The inventory will fit the individual. Perhaps this seems difficult or painful. It may appear impossible. We may fear that being in touch with our feelings will trigger an overwhelming chain reaction of pain and panic. We may feel like avoiding an inventory because of a fear of failure. When we ignore our feelings, the tension becomes too much for us. The fear of impending doom is so great that it overrides our fear of failure.

An inventory becomes a relief, because the pain of doing it is less than the pain of not doing it. We learn that pain can be a motivating factor in recovery. Thus, facing it becomes unavoidable. Every topic of step meetings seems to be on the Fourth Step or doing a daily inventory. Through the inventory process, we are able to deal with all the things that can build up. The more we live our program, the more God seems to put us in positions where issues surface. When issues surface, we write about them. We begin enjoying our recovery, because we have a way to resolve shame, guilt, or resentment.

The stress once trapped inside of us is released. Writing will lift the lid off of our pressure cooker. We decide whether we want to serve it up, put the lid back on it, or throw it out. We no longer have to stew in it.

We sit down with paper and pen and ask for our God's help in revealing the defects that are causing pain and suffering. We pray for the courage to be fearless and thorough and that this inventory may help us to put our lives in order. When we pray and take action, it always goes better for us.

We are not going to be perfect. If we were perfect, we would not be human. The important thing is that we do our best. We use the tools available to us, and we develop the ability to survive our emotions. We do not want to lose any of what we have gained; we want to continue in the program. It is our experience that no matter how searching and thorough, no inventory is of any lasting effect unless it is promptly followed by an equally thorough Fifth Step.

Step Five

"We admitted to God, to ourselves, and to another human being the exact nature of our wrongs."

The Fifth Step is the key to freedom. It allows us to live clean in the present. Sharing the exact nature of our wrongs sets us free to live. After taking a thorough Fourth Step, we deal with the contents of our inventory. We are told that if we keep these defects inside us, they will lead us back to using. Holding on to our past would eventually sicken us and keep us from taking part in our new way of life. If we are not honest when we take a Fifth Step, we will have the same negative results that dishonesty brought us in the past.

Step Five suggests that we admit to God, to ourselves, and to another human being the exact nature of our wrongs. We looked at our wrongs, examined our behavior patterns, and started to see the deeper aspects of our disease. Now we sit with another person and share our inventory out loud.

Our Higher Power will be with us during our Fifth Step. We will receive help and be free to face ourselves and another human being. It seemed unnecessary to admit the exact nature of our wrongs to our Higher Power. "God already knows that stuff," we rationalized. Although He already knows, the admission must come from our own lips to be truly effective. Step Five is not simply a reading of Step Four.

For years, we avoided seeing ourselves as we really were. We were ashamed of ourselves and felt isolated from the rest of the world. Now that we have the shameful part of our past trapped, we can sweep it out of our lives if we face and admit it. It would be tragic to write it all down and then shove it in a drawer. These defects grow in the dark, and die in the light of exposure.

Before coming to Narcotics Anonymous, we felt that no one could understand the things that we had done. We feared that if we ever revealed ourselves as we were, we would surely be rejected. Most addicts are uncomfortable about this. We recognize that we have been unrealistic in feeling this way. Our fellow members do understand us.

We must carefully choose the person who is to hear our Fifth Step. We must make sure that they know what we are doing and why we are doing it. Although there is no hard rule about the person of our choice, it is important that we trust the person. Only complete confidence in the person's integrity and discretion can make us willing to be thorough in this step. Some of us take our Fifth Step with a total stranger, although some of us feel more comfortable choosing a member of Narcotics Anonymous. We know that another addict would be less likely to judge us with malice or misunderstanding.

Once we make a choice and are actually alone with that person, we proceed with their encouragement. We want to be definite, honest, and thorough, realizing that this is a life and death matter.

Some of us tried to hide part of our past in an attempt to find an easier way of dealing with our inner feelings. We may think that we have done enough by writing about our past. We cannot afford this mistake. This step will expose our motives and our actions. We cannot expect these things to reveal themselves. Our embarrassment is eventually overcome, and we can avoid future guilt.

We do not procrastinate. We must be exact. We want to tell the simple truth, cut and dried, as quickly as possible. There is always a danger that we will exaggerate our wrongs. It is equally dangerous to minimize or rationalize our part in past situations. After all, we still want to sound good.

Addicts tend to live secret lives. For many years, we covered low self-esteem by hiding behind phony images that we hoped would fool people. Unfortunately, we fooled ourselves more than anyone.

Although we often appeared attractive and confident on the outside, we were really hiding a shaky, insecure person on the inside. The masks have to go. We share our inventory as it is written, skipping nothing. We continue to approach this step with honesty and thoroughness until we finish. It is a great relief to get rid of all our secrets and to share the burden of our past.

Usually, as we share this step, the listener will share some of his or her story too. We find that we are not unique. We see, by the acceptance of our confidant, that we can be accepted just the way we are.

We may never be able to remember all of our past mistakes. We do, however, give it our best and most complete effort. We begin to experience real personal feelings of a spiritual nature. Where once we had spiritual theories, we now begin to awaken to spiritual reality. This initial examination of ourselves usually reveals some behavior patterns that we don't particularly like. However, facing these patterns and bringing them out in the open makes it possible for us to deal with them constructively. We cannot make these changes alone. We will need the help of God, as we understand Him, and the Fellowship of Narcotics Anonymous.

Step Six

"We were entirely ready to have God remove all these defects of character."

Why ask for something before we are ready for it? This would be asking for trouble. So many times addicts have sought the rewards of hard work without the labor. Willingness is what we strive for in Step Six. How sincerely we work this step will be proportionate to our desire for change.

Do we really want to be rid of our resentments, our anger, our fear? Many of us cling to our fears, doubts, self-loathing, or hatred because there is a certain distorted security in familiar pain. It seems safer to embrace what we know than to let go of it for the unknown.

Letting go of character defects should be done decisively. We suffer because their demands weaken us. Where we were proud, we now find that we cannot get away with arrogance. If we are not humble, we are humiliated. If we are greedy, we find that we are never satisfied. Before taking Steps Four and Five, we could indulge in fear, anger, dishonesty, or self-pity. Now indulgence in these character defects clouds our ability to think logically. Selfishness becomes an intolerable, destructive chain that ties us to our bad habits. Our defects drain us of all our time and energy.

We examine the Fourth Step inventory and get a good look at what these defects are doing to our lives. We begin to long for freedom from these defects. We pray or otherwise become willing, ready, and able to let God remove these destructive traits. We need a personality change, if we are to stay clean. We want to change.

We should approach old defects with an open mind. We are aware of them and yet we still make the same mistakes and are unable to break the bad habits. We look to the fellowship for the kind of life that we want for ourselves. We ask our friends, "Did you let go?" Almost without exception the answer is, "Yes, to the best of my ability." When we see how our defects exist in our lives and accept them, we can let go of them and get on with our new life. We learn that we are growing when we make new mistakes instead of repeating old ones.

When we are working Step Six, it is important to remember that we are human and should not place unrealistic expectations on ourselves. This is a step of willingness. Willingness is the spiritual principle of Step Six. Step Six helps us move in a spiritual direction. Being human we will wander off course.

Rebellion is a character defect that spoils us here. We need not lose faith when we become rebellious. Rebellion can produce indifference or intolerance which can be overcome by persistent effort. We keep asking for willingness. We may be doubtful that God will see fit to relieve us or that something will go wrong. We ask another member who says, "You're right where you're supposed to be." We renew our readiness to have our defects removed. We surrender to the simple suggestions that the program offers us. Even though we are not entirely ready, we are headed in the right direction.

Eventually faith, humility, and acceptance replace pride and rebellion. We come to know ourselves. We find ourselves growing into mature consciousness. We begin to feel better, as willingness grows into hope. Perhaps for the first time, we see a vision of our new life. With this in sight, we put our willingness into action by moving on to Step Seven.

Step Seven

"We humbly asked Him to remove our shortcomings."

Character defects or shortcomings are those things that cause pain and misery all of our lives. If they contributed to our health and happiness, we would not have come to such a state of desperation. We had to become ready to have God, as we understood Him, remove these defects.

Having decided that we want God to relieve us of the useless or destructive aspects of our personalities, we have arrived at the Seventh Step. We couldn't handle the ordeal of life all by ourselves. It wasn't until we made a real mess of our lives that we realized we couldn't do it alone. By admitting this, we achieved a glimpse of humility. This is the main ingredient of Step Seven. Humility is a result of getting honest with ourselves. We have practiced being honest since Step One. We accepted our addiction and powerlessness. We found a strength beyond ourselves and learned to rely on it. We examined our lives and discovered who we really are. To be truly humble is to accept and honestly try to be ourselves. None of us is perfectly good or perfectly bad. We are people who have assets and liabilities. Most importantly, we are human.

Humility is as much a part of staying clean as food and water are to staying alive. As our addiction progressed, we devoted our energy toward satisfying our material desires. All other needs were beyond our reach. We always wanted gratification of our basic desires.

The Seventh Step is an action step, and it is time to ask God for help and relief. We have to understand that our way of thinking is not the only way; other people can give us direction. When someone points out a shortcoming, our first reaction may be defensive. We must realize that we are not perfect. There will always be room for growth. If we truly want to be free, we will take a good look at input from fellow addicts. If the shortcomings we discover are real, and we have a chance to be rid of them, we will surely experience a sense of well-being.

Some will want to get on their knees for this step. Some will be very quiet, and others will put forth a great emotional effort to show intense willingness. The word humble applies because we approach this Power greater than ourselves to ask for the freedom to live without the limitations of our past ways. Many of us are willing to work this step without reservations, on pure blind faith, because we are sick of what we have been doing and how we are feeling. Whatever works, we go all the way.

This is our road to spiritual growth. We change every day. We gradually and carefully pull ourselves out of the isolation and loneliness of addiction and into the mainstream of life. This growth is not the result of wishing, but of action and prayer. The main objective of Step Seven is to get out of ourselves and strive to achieve the will of our Higher Power.

If we are careless and fail to grasp the spiritual meaning of this step, we may have difficulties and stir up old troubles. One danger is in being too hard on ourselves.

Sharing with other recovering addicts will help us to avoid becoming morbidly serious about ourselves. Accepting the defects of others can help us become humble and pave the way for our own defects to be relieved. God often works through those who care enough about recovery to help make us aware of our shortcomings.

We have noticed that humility plays a big part in this program and our new way of life. We take our inventory; we become ready to let God remove our defects of character; we humbly ask Him to remove our shortcomings. This is our road to spiritual growth, and we will want to continue. We are ready for Step Eight.

Step Eight

"We made a list of all persons we had harmed, and became willing to make amends to them all."

Step Eight is the test of our newfound humility. Our purpose is to achieve freedom from the guilt that we have carried. We want to look the world in the eye with neither aggressiveness nor fear.

Are we willing to make a list of all persons we had harmed to clear away the fear and guilt that our past holds for us? Our experience tells us that we must become willing before this step will have any effect.

The Eighth Step is not easy; it demands a new kind of honesty about our relations with other people. The Eighth Step starts the process of forgiveness: We forgive others; possibly we are forgiven; and finally we forgive ourselves and learn how to live in the world. By the time we reach this step, we have become ready to understand rather than to be understood. We can live and let live easier when we know the areas in which we owe amends. It seems hard now, but once we have done it, we will wonder why we did not do it long ago.

We need some real honesty before we can make an accurate list. In preparing to make the Eighth Step list, it is helpful to define harm. One definition of harm is physical or mental damage. Another definition of harm is inflicting pain, suffering, or loss. The damage may be caused by something that is said, done, or left undone. Harm can result from words or actions, either intentional or unintentional. The degree of harm can range from making someone feel mentally uncomfortable to inflicting bodily injury or even death.

The Eighth Step presents us with a problem. Many of us have difficulty admitting that we caused harm for others, because we thought we were victims of our addiction. Avoiding this rationalization is crucial to the Eighth Step. We must separate what was done to us from what we did to others. We cut away our justifications and our ideas of being a victim. We often feel that we only harmed ourselves, yet we usually list ourselves last, if at all. This step is doing the legwork to repair the wreckage of our lives.

It will not make us better people to judge the faults of another. It will make us feel better to cleanup our lives by relieving ourselves of guilt. By writing our list, we can no longer deny that we caused harm. We admit that we hurt others, directly or indirectly, through some action, lie, broken promise, or neglect.

We make our list, or take it from our Fourth Step, and add additional people as we think of them. We face this list honestly, and openly examine our faults so we can become willing to make amends.

In some cases, we may not know the persons that we have wronged. While using, anyone that we contacted was at risk. Many members mention their parents, spouses, children, friends, lovers, other addicts, casual acquaintances, co-workers, employers, teachers, landlords, and total strangers. We may also place ourselves on the list, because while practicing our addiction, we have slowly been killing ourselves. We may find it beneficial to make a separate list of people to whom we owe financial amends.

As with each step, we must be thorough. Most of us fall short of our goals more often than we exceed them. At the same time, we cannot put off completion of this step just because we are not sure that our list is complete. We are never finished.

The final difficulty in working the Eighth Step is separating it from the Ninth Step. Projections about actually making amends can be a major obstacle both in making the list and in becoming willing. We do this step as if there were no Ninth Step. We do not even think about making the amends, but just concentrate on exactly what the Eighth Step says: make a list and become willing. The main thing this step does for us is to help build awareness that, little by little, we are gaining new attitudes about ourselves and how we deal with other people.

Listening carefully to other members share their experience regarding this step can relieve any confusion that we may have about writing our list. Also, our sponsors may share with us how Step Eight worked for them. Asking a question during a meeting can give us the benefit of group conscience.

The Eighth Step offers a big change from a life dominated by guilt and remorse. Our futures are changed, because we don't have to avoid those who we have harmed. As a result of this step, we receive a new freedom that can end isolation. As we realize our need to be forgiven, we tend to be more forgiving. At least, we know that we are no longer intentionally making life miserable for people.

The Eighth Step is an action step. Like all the steps, it offers immediate benefits. We are now free to begin our amends in Step Nine.

Step Nine

"We made direct amends to such people wherever possible, except when to do so would injure them or others."

This step should not be avoided. If we do, we are reserving a place in our program for relapse. Pride, fear and procrastination often seem an impossible barrier; they stand in the way of progress and growth. The important thing is to take action and to be ready to accept the reactions of those persons we have harmed. We make amends to the best of our ability.

Timing is an essential part of this step. We should make amends when the opportunity presents itself, except when to do so will cause more harm. Sometimes we cannot actually make the amends; it is neither possible nor practical. In some cases, amends may be beyond our means. We find that willingness can serve in the place of action where we are unable to contact the person that we have harmed. However, we should never fail to contact anyone because of embarrassment, fear, or procrastination.

We want to be free of our guilt, but we don't wish to do so at the expense of anyone else. We might run the risk of involving a third person or some companion from our using days who does not wish to be exposed. We do not have the right or the need to endanger another person. It is often necessary to take guidance from others in these matters.

We recommend turning our legal problems over to lawyers and our financial or medical problems to professionals. Part of learning how to live successfully is learning when we need help.

In some old relationships, an unresolved conflict may still exist. We do our part to resolve old conflicts by making our amends. We want to step away from further antagonisms and ongoing resentments. In many instances, we can only go to the person and humbly ask for understanding of past wrongs. Sometimes this will be a joyous occasion when old friends or relatives prove willing to let go of their bitterness. Contacting someone who is still hurting from the burn of our misdeeds can be dangerous. Indirect amends may be necessary where direct ones would be unsafe or endanger other people. We make our amends to the best of our ability. We try to remember that when we make amends, we are doing it for ourselves. Instead of feeling guilty and remorseful, we feel relieved about our past.

We accept that it was our actions that caused our negative attitude. Step Nine helps us with our guilt and helps others with their anger. Sometimes, the only amend we can make is to stay clean. We owe it to ourselves and to our loved ones. We are no longer making a mess in society as a result of our using. Sometimes the only way we can make amends is to contribute to society. Now, we are helping ourselves and other addicts to recover. This is a tremendous amend to the whole community.

In the process of our recovery, we are restored to sanity and part of sanity is effectively relating to others. We less often view people as a threat to our security. Real security will replace the physical ache and mental confusion that we have experienced in the past. We approach those we have harmed with humility and patience. Many of our sincere well-wishers may be reluctant to accept our recovery as real. We must remember the pain that they have known. In time, many miracles will occur. Many of us who were separated from our families succeed in establishing relationships with them. Eventually it becomes easier for them to accept the change in us. Clean time speaks for itself. Patience is an important part of our recovery. The unconditional love we experience will rejuvenate our will to live, and each positive move on our part will be matched by an unexpected opportunity. A lot of courage and faith goes into making an amend, and a lot of spiritual growth results.

We are achieving freedom from the wreckage of our past. We will want to keep our house in order by practicing a continuous personal inventory in Step Ten.

Step Ten

"We continued to take personal inventory and when we were wrong promptly admitted it."

Step Ten frees us from the wreckage of our present. If we do not stay aware of our defects, they can drive us into a corner that we can't get out of clean.

One of the first things we learn in Narcotics Anonymous is that if we use, we lose. By the same token, we won't experience as much pain if we can avoid the things that cause us pain. Continuing to take a personal inventory means that we form a habit of looking at ourselves, our actions, attitudes, and relationships on a regular basis.

We are creatures of habit and are vulnerable to our old ways of thinking and reacting. At times it seems easier to continue in the old rut of self-destruction than to attempt a new and seemingly dangerous route. We don't have to be trapped by our old patterns. Today, we have a choice.

The Tenth Step can help us correct our living problems and prevent their recurrence. We examine our actions during the day. Some of us write about our feelings, explaining how we felt and what part we might have played in any problems which occurred. Did we cause someone harm? Do we need to admit that we were wrong? If we find difficulties, we make an effort to take care of them. When these things are left undone, they have away of festering.

This step can be a defense against the old insanity. We can ask ourselves if we are being drawn into old patterns of anger, resentment, or fear. Do we feel trapped? Are we setting ourselves up for trouble? Are we too hungry, angry, lonely, or tired? Are we taking ourselves too seriously?

Are we judging our insides by the outside appearances of others? Do we suffer from some physical problem? The answers to these questions can help us deal with the difficulties of the moment. We no longer have to live with the feeling that we have a "hole in the gut." A lot of our chief concerns and major difficulties come from our inexperience with living without drugs. Often when we ask an oldtimer what to do, we are amazed at the simplicity of the answer.

The Tenth Step can be a pressure relief valve. We work this step while the day's ups and downs are still fresh in our minds. We list what we have done and try not to rationalize our actions. This may be done in writing at the end of the day. The first thing we do is stop! Then we take the time to allow ourselves the privilege of thinking. We examine our actions, reactions, and motives. We often find that we've been doing better than we've been feeling. This allows us to examine our actions and admit fault, before things get any worse. We need to avoid rationalizing. We promptly admit our faults, not explain them.

We work this step continuously. This is a preventive action. The more we work this step the less we will need the corrective part of this step. This step is a great tool for avoiding grief before we bring it on ourselves. We monitor our feelings, emotions, fantasies, and actions. By constantly looking at ourselves, we are able to avoid repeating the actions that make us feel bad.

We need this step even when we're feeling good and when things are going well. Good feelings are new to us, and we need to nurture them. In times of trouble, we can try the things that worked during the good times. We have the right to feel good. We have a choice. The good times can also be a trap; the danger is that we may forget that our first priority is to stay clean. For us, recovery is more than just pleasure.

We need to remember that everyone makes mistakes. We will never be perfect.

However, we can accept ourselves by using Step Ten. By continuing a personal inventory, we are set free, in the here and now, from ourselves and the past. We no longer justify our existence. This step allows us to be ourselves.

Step Eleven

"We sought through prayer and meditation to improve our conscious contact with God as we understood Him, *praying only for knowledge of His will for us and the power to carry that out."*

The first ten steps have set the stage for us to improve our conscious contact with the God of our understanding. They give us the foundation to achieve our long-sought, positive goals. Having entered this phase of our spiritual program through practicing the previous ten steps, most of us welcome the exercise of prayer and meditation. Our spiritual condition is the basis for a successful recovery that offers unlimited growth.

Many of us really begin to appreciate our recovery when we get to the Eleventh Step. In the Eleventh Step, our lives take on a deeper meaning. By surrendering control, we gain a far greater power.

The nature of our belief will determine the manner of our prayers and meditations. We need only make sure that we have a system of belief that works for us. Results count in recovery. As has been noted elsewhere, our prayers seemed to work as soon as we entered the program of Narcotics Anonymous and we surrendered to our disease. The conscious contact described in this step is the direct result of living the steps. We use this step to improve and maintain our spiritual condition.

When we first came into the program, we received help from a Power greater than ourselves. This was set in motion by our surrender to the program. The purpose of the Eleventh Step is to increase our awareness of that Power and to improve our ability to use it as a source of strength in our new lives.

The more we improve our conscious contact with our God through prayer and meditation, the easier it is to say, "Your will, not mine, be done." We can ask for God's help when we need it, and our lives get better. The experiences that some people talk about regarding meditation and individual religious beliefs don't always apply to us. Ours is a spiritual, not a religious program. By the time we get to the Eleventh Step, character defects that caused problems in the past have been addressed by working the preceding ten steps. The image of the kind of person that we would like to be is a fleeting glimpse of God's will for us. Often, our outlook is so limited that we can only see our immediate wants and needs.

It is easy to slip back into our old ways. To ensure our continued growth and recovery, we have to learn to maintain our lives on a spiritually sound basis. God will not force His goodness on us, but we will receive it if we ask. We usually feel something is different in the moment, but don't see the change in our lives till later. When we finally get our own selfish motives out of the way, we begin to find a peace that we never imagined possible. Enforced morality lacks the power that comes to us when we choose to live a spiritual life. Most of us pray when we are hurting. We learn that if we pray regularly, we won't be hurting as often or as intensely.

Outside of Narcotics Anonymous, there are any number of different groups practicing meditation. Nearly all of these groups are connected with a particular religion or philosophy. An endorsement of any one of these methods would be a violation of our traditions and a restriction on the individual's right to have a God of his understanding. Meditation allows us to develop spiritually in our own way. Some of the things that didn't work for us in the past, might work today. We take a fresh look at each day with an open mind. We know that if we pray for God's will, we will receive what is best for us, regardless of what we think. This knowledge is based on our belief and experience as recovering addicts.

Prayer is communicating our concerns to a Power greater than ourselves. Sometimes when we pray, a remarkable thing happens; we find the means, ways, and energies to perform tasks far beyond our capacities. We grasp the limitless strength provided for us through our daily prayer and surrender, as long as we keep faith and renew it.

For some, prayer is asking for God's help; meditation is listening for God's answer. We learn to be careful of praying for specific things. We pray that God will show us His will, and that He will help us carry that out. In some cases, he makes His will so obvious to us that we have little difficulty seeing it. In others, our egos are so self-centered that we won't accept God's will for us without another struggle and surrender. If we pray for God to remove any distracting influences, the quality of our prayers usually improves and we feel the difference. Prayer takes practice, and we should remind ourselves that skilled people were not born with their skills. It took lots of effort on their part to develop them. Through prayer, we seek conscious contact with our God. In meditation, we achieve this contact, and the Eleventh Step helps us to maintain it.

We may have been exposed to many religions and meditative disciplines before coming to Narcotics Anonymous. Some of us were devastated and completely confused by these practices. We were sure that it was God's will for us to use drugs to reach higher consciousness. Many of us found ourselves in very strange states as a result of these practices. We never suspected the damaging effects of our addiction as the root of our difficulty and pursued to the end whatever path offered hope.

In quiet moments of meditation, God's will can become evident to us. Quieting the mind through meditation brings an inner peace that brings us into contact with the God within us. A basic premise of meditation is that it is difficult, if not impossible, to obtain conscious contact unless our mind is still. The usual, never-ending succession of thoughts has to cease for progress to be made. So our preliminary practice is aimed at stilling the mind, and letting the thoughts that arise die a natural death. We leave our thoughts behind as the meditation part of the Eleventh Step becomes a reality for us.

Emotional balance is one of the first results of meditation, and our experience bears this out. Some of us came into the program broken, and hung around for awhile, only to find God or salvation in one kind of religious cult or another. It is easy to float back out the door on a cloud of religious zeal and forget that we are addicts with an incurable disease.

It is said that for meditation to be of value, the results must show in our daily lives. This fact is implicit in the Eleventh Step: "… His will for us and the power to carry it out." For those of us who do not pray, meditation is our only way of working this step.

We find ourselves praying, because it brings us peace and restores our confidence and courage. It helps us to live a life that is free of fear and distrust. When we remove our selfish motives and pray for guidance, we find feelings of peace and serenity. We begin to experience an awareness and an empathy with other people that was not possible before working this step.

As we seek our personal contact with God, we begin to open up as a flower in the sun. We begin to see that God's love has been present all the time, just waiting for us to accept it. We do the footwork and accept what's being given to us freely on a daily basis. We find relying on God becomes more comfortable for us.

When we first come to the program, we usually ask for a lot of things that seem to be important wants and needs. As we grow spiritually and find a Power greater than ourselves, we begin to realize that as long as our spiritual needs are met, our living problems are reduced to a point of comfort. When we forget where our real strength lies, we quickly become subject to the same patterns of thinking and action that got us to the program in the first place. We eventually redefine our beliefs and understanding to the point where we see that our greatest need is for knowledge of God's will for us and the strength to carry that out. We are able to set aside some of our personal preference, because we learn that God's will for us consists of the very things we most value. God's will for us becomes our own true will for ourselves. This happens in an intuitive manner that cannot be adequately explained in words.

We become willing to let other people be who they are without having to pass judgment on them. The urgency to take care of things isn't there anymore. We couldn't comprehend acceptance in the beginning; today, we can.

We know that whatever the day brings, God has given us everything we need for our spiritual well-being. It is all right for us to admit powerlessness, because God is powerful enough to help us stay clean and to enjoy spiritual progress. God is helping us to get our house in order.

We begin to see more clearly what is real. Through constant contact with our Higher Power, the answers that we seek come to us. We gain the ability to do what we once could not. We respect the beliefs of others. We encourage you to seek strength and guidance according to your belief.

We are thankful for this step, because we begin to get what is best for us. Sometimes, we prayed for our wants and got trapped once we got them. We could pray and get something, then have to pray for its removal, because we couldn't handle it.

Hopefully, having learned the power of prayer and the responsibility prayer brings with it, we can use the Eleventh Step as a guideline for our daily program.

We begin to pray only for God's will for us. This way, we are getting only what we are capable of handling. We are able to respond to it and handle it, because

God helps us prepare for it. Some of us simply use our words to give thanks for God's grace.

In an attitude of surrender and humility, we approach this step again and again to receive the gift of knowledge and strength from the God of our understanding. The Tenth Step clears away the errors of the present so we may work the Eleventh Step. Without this step, it is unlikely that we could experience a spiritual awakening, practice spiritual principles in our lives, or carry a sufficient message to attract others to recovery. There is a spiritual principle of giving away what we have been given in Narcotics Anonymous in order to keep it. By helping others to stay clean, we enjoy the benefit of the spiritual wealth that we have found. We must give freely and gratefully that which has been freely and gratefully given to us.

Step Twelve

"Having had a spiritual awakening as a result of these steps, we tried to carry this message to addicts, and to practice these principles in all our affairs."

We came to Narcotics Anonymous as the result of the wreckage of our past. The last thing we expected was an awakening of the spirit. We just wanted to stop hurting.

The steps lead to an awakening of a spiritual nature. This awakening is evidenced by changes in our lives. These changes make us better able to live by spiritual principles and to carry our message of recovery and hope to the addict who still suffers. The message, however, is meaningless unless we LIVE it. As we live it, our lives and actions give it more meaning than our words and literature ever could.

The idea of a spiritual awakening takes many different forms in the different personalities that we find in the fellowship. However, all spiritual awakenings have some things in common. Common elements include an end to loneliness and a sense of direction in our lives. Many of us believe that a spiritual awakening is meaningless unless accompanied by an increase in peace of mind and a concern for others. In order to maintain peace of mind, we strive to live in the here and now.

Those of us who have worked these steps to the best of our ability received many benefits. We believe that these benefits are a direct result of living this program.

When we first begin to enjoy relief from our addiction, we run the risk of assuming control of our lives again. We forget the agony and pain that we have known. Our disease controlled our lives when we were using. It is ready and waiting to take over again. We quickly forget that all our past efforts at controlling our lives failed.

By this time, most of us realize that the only way that we can keep what was given to us is by sharing this new gift of life with the still-suffering addict. This is our best insurance against relapse to the torturous existence of using. We call it carrying the message, and we do it in a number of ways.

In the Twelfth Step, we practice the spiritual principles of giving the NA message of recovery in order to keep it. Even a member with one day in the NA Fellowship can carry the message that this program works.

When we share with someone new, we may ask to be used as a spiritual instrument of our Higher Power. We don't set ourselves up as gods. We often ask for the help of another recovering addict when sharing with a new person. It is a privilege to respond to a cry for help. We, who have been in the pits of despair, feel fortunate to help others find recovery.

We help new people learn the principles of Narcotics Anonymous. We try to make them feel welcome and help them learn what the program has to offer. We share our experience, strength, and hope. Whenever possible, we accompany newcomers to a meeting.

The selfless service of this work is the very principle of Step Twelve. We received our recovery from the God of our understanding. We now make ourselves available as His tool to share recovery with those who seek it. Most of us learn that we can only carry our message to someone who is asking for help. Sometimes, the only message necessary to make the suffering addict reach out is the power of example. An addict may be suffering but unwilling to ask for help. We can make ourselves available to these people, so when they ask, someone will be there.

Learning to help others is a benefit of the Narcotics Anonymous program. Remarkably, working the Twelve Steps guides us from humiliation and despair to acting as instruments of our Higher Power. We are given the ability to help a fellow addict when no one else can. We see it happening among us every day. This miraculous turnabout is evidence of spiritual awakening. We share from our own personal experience what it has been like for us. The temptation to give advice is great, but when we do so we lose the respect of newcomers. This clouds our message. A simple, honest message of recovery from addiction rings true.

We attend meetings and make ourselves visible and available to serve the fellowship. We give freely and gratefully of our time, service, and what we have found here. The service we speak of in Narcotics Anonymous is the primary purpose of our groups. Service work is carrying the message to the addict who still suffers. The more eagerly we wade in and work, the richer our spiritual awakening will be.

The first way that we carry the message speaks for itself. People see us on the street and remember us as devious, frightened loners. They notice the fear leaving our faces. They see us gradually come alive.

Once we find the NA way, boredom and complacency have no place in our new life. By staying clean, we begin to practice spiritual principles such as hope, surrender, acceptance, honesty, open-mindedness, willingness, faith, tolerance, patience, humility, unconditional love, sharing, and caring. As our recovery progresses, spiritual principles touch every area of our lives, because we simply try to live this program in the here and now.

We find joy as we start to learn how to live by the principles of recovery. It is the joy of watching as a person two days clean says to a person with one day clean, "An addict alone is in bad company." It is the joy of watching a person who was struggling to make it suddenly, in the middle of helping another addict to stay clean, become able to find the words needed to carry the message of recovery.

We feel that our lives have become worthwhile. Spiritually refreshed, we are glad to be alive. When we were using, our lives became an exercise in survival. Now we are doing much more living than surviving. Realizing that the bottom line is staying clean, we can enjoy life. We like being clean and enjoy carrying the message of recovery to the addict who still suffers. Going to meetings really works.

Practicing spiritual principles in our daily lives leads us to a new image of ourselves. Honesty, humility, and open-mindedness help us to treat our associates fairly. Our decisions become tempered with tolerance. We learn to respect ourselves.

The lessons we learn in our recovery are sometimes bitter and painful. By helping others we find the reward of self-respect, as we are able to share these lessons with other members of Narcotics Anonymous. We cannot deny other addicts their pain, but we can carry the message of hope that was given to us by fellow addicts in recovery. We share the principles of recovery, as they have worked in our lives. God helps us as we help each other. Life takes on a new meaning, a new joy, and a quality of being and feeling worthwhile. We become spiritually refreshed and are glad to be alive. One aspect of our spiritual awakening comes through the new understanding of our Higher Power that we develop by sharing another addict's recovery.

Yes, we are a vision of hope. We are examples of the program working. The joy that we have in living clean is an attraction to the addict who still suffers.

We do recover to live clean and happy lives. Welcome to NA. The steps do not end here. The steps are a new beginning!

Self-Acceptance

The problem

The lack of self-acceptance is a problem for many recovering addicts. This subtle defect is difficult to identify and often goes unrecognized. Many of us believed that using drugs was our only problem, denying the fact that our lives had become unmanageable. Even after we stop using, this denial can continue to plague us. Many of the problems we experience in ongoing recovery stem from an inability to accept ourselves on a deep level. We may not even realize that this discomfort is the source of our problem, because it is often manifested in other ways. We may find ourselves becoming irritable or judgmental, discontent, depressed, or confused. We may find ourselves trying to change environmental factors in an attempt to satisfy the inner gnawing we feel. In situations such as these our experience has shown that it is best to look inward for the source of our discontent. Very often, we discover that we are harsh critics of ourselves, wallowing in self-loathing and self-rejection.

Before coming to NA, most of us spent our entire lives in self-rejection. We hated ourselves and tried every way we could to become someone different. We wanted to be anyone but who we were. Unable to accept ourselves, we tried to gain the acceptance of others. We wanted other people to give us the love and acceptance we could not give ourselves, but our love and friendship were always conditional. We would do anything for anyone just to gain their acceptance and approval, and then would resent those who wouldn't respond the way we wanted them to.

Because we could not accept ourselves, we expected to be rejected by others. We would not allow anyone to get close to us for fear that if they really knew us, they would also hate us. To protect ourselves from vulnerability, we would reject others before they had a chance to reject us.

The Twelve Steps are the solution

Today, the first step toward self-acceptance is acceptance of our addiction. We must accept our disease and all the troubles that it brings us before we can accept ourselves as human beings.

The next thing we need to help us toward self-acceptance is belief in a Power greater than ourselves who can restore us to sanity. We do not need to believe in any particular person's concept of that Higher Power, but we do need to believe in a concept that works for us. A spiritual understanding of self-acceptance is knowing that it is all right to find ourselves in pain, to have made mistakes, and to know that we are not perfect.

The most effective means of achieving self-acceptance is through applying the Twelve Steps of recovery. Now that we have come to believe in a Power greater than ourselves, we can depend upon His strength to give us the courage to honestly examine our defects and our assets. Although it is sometimes painful and may not seem to lead to self-acceptance, it is necessary to get in touch with our feelings. We wish to build a solid foundation of recovery, and therefore need to examine our actions and motivations and begin changing those things that are unacceptable.

Our defects are part of us and will only be removed when we practice living the NA program. Our assets are gifts from our Higher Power, and as we learn to utilize them fully, our self-acceptance grows and our lives improve.

Sometimes we slip into the melodrama of wishing we could be what we think we should be. We may feel overpowered by our self-pity and pride, but by renewing our faith in a Higher Power we are given the hope, courage, and strength to grow.

Self-acceptance permits balance in our recovery. We no longer have to look for the approval of others because we are satisfied with being ourselves. We are free to gratefully emphasize our assets, to humbly move away from our defects, and to become the best recovering addicts we can be. Accepting ourselves as we are means that we are all right, that we are not perfect, but we can improve.

We remember that we have the disease of addiction, and that it takes a long time to achieve self-acceptance on a deep level. No matter how bad our lives have become, we are always accepted in the Fellowship of Narcotics Anonymous.

Accepting ourselves as we are resolves the problem of expecting human perfection. When we accept ourselves, we can accept others into our lives, unconditionally, probably for the first time. Our friendships become deep and we experience the warmth and caring which results from addicts sharing recovery and a new life.

**God, grant me the serenity
to accept the things I cannot change,
the courage to change the things I can,
and the wisdom to know the difference.**

Sponsorship, Revised

One of the first suggestions many of us hear when we begin attending NA meetings is to get a sponsor. As newcomers, we may not understand what this means. What is a sponsor? How do we get and use one? Where do we find one? This pamphlet is intended to serve as a brief introduction to sponsorship.

Our Basic Text tells us that "the heart of NA beats when two addicts share their recovery," and sponsorship is simply one addict helping another. The two-way street of sponsorship is a loving, spiritual, and compassionate relationship that helps both the sponsor and sponsee.

WHO is a sponsor?

Sponsorship is a personal and private relationship that can mean different things to different people. For the purposes of this pamphlet, an NA sponsor is a member of Narcotics Anonymous, living our program of recovery, who is willing to build a special, supportive, one-on-one relationship with us. Most members think of a sponsor, first and foremost, as someone who can help us work the Twelve Steps of NA, and sometimes the Twelve Traditions and Twelve Concepts. A sponsor is not necessarily a friend, but may be someone in whom we confide. We can share things with our sponsor that we might not be comfortable sharing in a meeting.

> "My relationship with my sponsor has been the key to gaining trust in other people and working the steps. I shared the total mess that was my life with my sponsor, and he shared that he had been in the same place. He began to teach me how to live without the use of drugs."

WHAT does a sponsor do?

Sponsors share their experience, strength, and hope with their sponsees. Some describe their sponsor as loving and compassionate, someone they can count on to listen and support them no matter what. Others value the objectivity and detachment a sponsor can offer, relying on their direct and honest input even when it may be difficult to accept. Still others turn to a sponsor mainly for guidance through the Twelve Steps.

> "Someone once asked, 'Why do I need a sponsor?' The sponsor replied, 'Well it's pretty hard to spot self deception... by yourself.'"

Sponsorship works for the same reason that NA works—because recovering members share common bonds of addiction and recovery and, in many cases, can empathize with each other. A sponsor's role is not that of a legal advisor, a banker, a parent, a marriage counselor, or a social worker. Nor is a sponsor a therapist offering some sort of professional advice. A sponsor is simply another addict in recovery who is willing to share his or her journey through the Twelve Steps.

As we share our concerns and questions with our sponsors, sometimes they will share their own experiences. At other times they may suggest reading or writing assignments, or try to answer our questions about the program. When we are new to NA, a sponsor can help us understand things that may confuse us about the program, from NA language, meeting formats, and the service structure, to the meaning of NA principles and the nature of spiritual awakening.

WHAT does a sponsee do?

One suggestion is to have regular contact with our sponsor. In addition to phoning our sponsor, we can arrange to meet up at meetings. Some sponsors will tell us how often they expect us to contact them, while others don't set those kinds of requirements. If we cannot find a sponsor who lives close to us, we can look to technology or mail to keep in touch. Regardless of how we communicate with our sponsor, it is important that we be honest and that we listen with an open mind.

> "I rely on my sponsor to give me general direction and a new perspective. If nothing else, she's an important sounding board. Sometimes all it takes is saying something out loud to someone else for me to see things differently."

We may worry that we are a burden to our sponsors and hesitate to contact them, or we may believe our sponsors will want something in return from us. But the truth is our sponsors benefit as much as we do from the relationship. In our program, we believe that we can only keep what we have by giving it away; by using our sponsors, we are actually helping them to stay clean and recover.

HOW do we get a sponsor?

To get a sponsor, all we need to do is ask. While this is simple, it may not be easy. Many of us are afraid to ask someone to be our sponsor. In active addiction, we may have learned not to trust anyone, and the idea of asking someone to listen to us and help us may feel alien and frightening. Nonetheless, most of our members describe sponsorship as a crucial part of their recovery. Sometimes we finally gather our courage, only to have someone say no. If that happens, we need to be persistent, have faith, and try not to take his or her decision personally. The reasons people may decline probably have nothing to do with us: they may have busy lives or many sponsees, or they may be going through difficult times. We need to reaffirm our faith and ask someone else.

> "When I picked my sponsor, I looked at it like an interview. Are we a match? What are your expectations and what are mine? I looked for someone open-minded who I felt comfortable talking to."

The best place to look for a sponsor is at an NA meeting. Other places to seek a sponsor are NA events, such as service meetings and conventions. In seeking a sponsor, most members look for someone they feel they can learn to trust, someone who seems compassionate and who is active in the program. Most members, particularly those who are new to NA, consider it important to find a sponsor with more clean time than they have.

A good rule of thumb is to look for someone with similar experiences who can relate to our struggles and accomplishments. For most, finding a sponsor of the same sex makes this empathy easier and helps us feel safe in the relationship. Some feel gender need not be a deciding factor. We are free to choose our own sponsor. It is, however, strongly suggested that we avoid getting into a sponsorship relationship that may lead to sexual attraction. Such attraction can distract us from the nature of sponsorship and interfere with our ability to share honestly with each other.

> "When I got clean, I was insecure, lonely, and willing to do anything for some comfort and company. My natural tendency was to satisfy those desires and not have to focus on what was necessary to build a foundation for my recovery. Thank God for the integrity of those members who supported me and didn't take advantage of me in the early days of my recovery."

Sometimes members wonder whether it would be okay to have more than one sponsor. While some addicts do choose this route, most caution against it, explaining that having more than one sponsor might tempt them to be manipulative in order to get the answers or guidance they are looking for.

WHEN should we get a sponsor?

Most members consider it important to get a sponsor as soon as possible, while others explain that it is just as crucial to take a little time to look around and make an informed decision. Going to a lot of meetings helps us to determine who we are comfortable with and who we can learn to trust. While we are looking for a sponsor, if someone offers, we do not have to say yes. One thing to remember is that, if we get a sponsor to help us in our early recovery, we are free to change sponsors later if that person isn't meeting our needs.

> "I compared the timing of when to get a sponsor to drowning. I needed that life-saver/sponsor immediately!"

When we are new to the program, we need to reach out to other addicts for help and support. It is never too early to get and use phone numbers and begin sharing with other recovering addicts. Our program works because of the help we can offer each other. We no longer need to live in isolation, and we begin to feel part of something larger than ourselves. Sponsorship helps us to see that, in coming to NA, we have finally come home.

You may have questions about sponsorship that this IP did not answer for you. While there may not be "right" or "wrong" answers to your questions—the experience of our fellowship varies from community to community and member to member—we do have a book on sponsorship that addresses many issues related to sponsorship in greater depth.

One Addict's Experience with Acceptance, Faith, and Commitment

When I came on the NA program, I had identified my problem—I had the desire to stop using, but couldn't see how. Due to the nature of addiction my whole personality was geared toward getting, using, and finding ways and means to get more. All of my personality traits reinforced this obsession with self. Totally self-centered, I tried to manage my life by manipulating people and circumstances to my advantage. I had lost all control. Obsession forced me to use drugs repeatedly, against my will, knowing that it was self-destructive, and against my basic instinct for survival. Insane, and feeling hopelessly helpless, I gave up fighting, and accepted that I was an addict—that my life was totally unmanageable, and that I was powerless over the disease. My willpower could not change my diseased body that craved drugs compulsively. My self-control could not change my diseased mind, obsessed with the idea of using mood changers to escape reality. Nor could my highest ideals change my diseased spirit—cunning, insidious, and totally self-centered. As soon as I was able to accept the reality of my powerlessness, I no longer needed to use drugs. This acceptance of my condition—my powerlessness over addiction and the unmanageability of my life was the key to my recovery.

With the help of the recovering addicts at NA meetings, I abstained—a minute, an hour, a day at a time. I still wanted to get high. Life felt intolerable without drugs. Giving up left me feeling even more hopeless than before, and, to cope, my mind told me to use drugs again. Acceptance of my powerlessness and the unmanageability of my life left me needing a power stronger than my disease to change my self-destructive nature. The people I met at meetings told me they had found a power greater than their addiction in the NA program. These people had been clean for months or years and didn't even want to use any more. They told me that I could lose the desire to use drugs by living the NA program. I had no choice but to believe them. I had tried doctors, psychiatrists, hospitals, mental institutions, job changes, marriages, divorces; all had failed. It seemed hopeless, but in NA I saw hope. I met addicts recovering from their disease. I came to believe I could learn how to live without drugs. In NA, I found the faith I needed to begin to change.

At that point, I had stopped using drugs and reluctantly believed that I could continue to abstain. I still thought and felt like an addict, I just didn't use drugs. My personality and character were the same as they had always been. Everything about me reinforced my self-destructiveness. I needed to change or I would start to use again. I had accepted my condition and believed that I could recover. In order to do so, I had to make a total commitment to the spiritual principles of the NA program.

With the help of my sponsor, I decided to turn my life and my will over to God, as I understood God. For me, this was a turning point. This decision demanded continued acceptance, ever-increasing faith, and a daily commitment to recovery. The decision to turn my life and will over to God required that I find out about myself and actively try to change my ways of coping with reality. This commitment brought honesty into my life. This is how the NA program works for me: I accept my disease, develop a faith that the program can change me, and make a commitment to the spiritual principles of recovery.

Action is now required. If I don't change, I will be miserable and return to using drugs. The actions suggested by the NA program can change my personality and character. I honestly examine myself, writing down what I have done and how

I have felt. I reveal myself completely to my God and to another human being, telling all of my most secret fears, angers, and resentments. By doing these things, the past no longer has control over my life, and I am freed to live up to my ideals today. I begin to behave differently and become ready to be changed by my God into the sort of person He wants me to be.

I have begun to develop a reasonable self-image, based in reality, by asking to be relieved of my shortcomings.

By amending the wrongs I have done to other people, I have learned how to forgive myself and others.

I review my behavior regularly and correct my mistakes as soon as possible. I am continually developing and expanding trust and faith in spiritual principles. I give to others, sharing myself, and our program, and try to live the principles that I learned. These Twelve Steps have allowed me to stop using, have taken away the desire to use, and have given me a new way of life.

Just for Today

Tell yourself:

Just for today, my thoughts will be on my recovery, living and enjoying life without the use of drugs.

Just for today, I will have faith in someone in NA who believes in me and wants to help me in my recovery.

Just for today, I will have a program. I will try to follow it to the best of my ability.

Just for today, through NA, I will try to get a better perspective on my life.

Just for today, I will be unafraid. My thoughts will be on my new associations, people who are not using and who have found a new way of life. So long as I follow that way, I have nothing to fear.

When we came into the program of Narcotics Anonymous, we made a decision to turn our lives over to the care of a Higher Power. This surrender relieves the burden of the past and fear of the future. The gift of today is now in proper perspective. We accept and enjoy life as it is right now. When we refuse to accept the reality of today, we are denying our faith in our Higher Power. This can only bring more suffering.

We learn that today is a gift with no guarantees. With this in mind, the insignificance of the past and future, and the importance of our actions today, become real for us. This simplifies our lives.

When we focus our thoughts on today, the nightmare of drugs fades away overshadowed by the dawn of a new reality. We find that, when we are troubled, we can trust our feelings to another recovering addict. In sharing our past with other addicts we discover we are not unique, that we share common bonds. Talking to other NA members, whether to share the trials and tribulations of our day with them, or allowing them to share theirs with us, is a way our Higher Power works through us.

We have no need to fear if today we stay clean, close to our Higher Power and our NA friends. God has forgiven us for our past mistakes, and tomorrow is not yet here. Meditation and a personal inventory will help us to gain serenity and guidance throughout this day. We take a few moments out of our daily routine to thank God, as we understand God, for giving us the ability to cope with today.

"Just for today" applies to all areas of our lives, not just abstinence from drugs. Reality has to be dealt with on a daily basis. Many of us feel that God expects no more of us than to do the things that we are able to do today.

Working the program, the Twelve Steps of NA, has given us a new outlook on our lives. Today, we no longer need to make excuses for who we are. Our daily contact with a Higher Power fills the empty places inside that could never be filled before. We find fulfillment in living today. With our Higher Power guiding us, we lose the desire to use. Perfection is no longer a goal today; we can achieve adequacy.

It is important to remember that any addict who can stay clean for one day is a miracle. Going to meetings, working the steps, daily meditation, and talking with people in the program are things we do to stay spiritually healthy. Responsible living is possible.

We can replace loneliness and fear with the love of the fellowship and the security of a new way of life. We never have to be alone again. In the fellowship, we have made more true friends than we ever believed possible. Self-pity and resentments are replaced by tolerance and faith. We are given the freedom, serenity, and happiness we so desperately sought.

A lot happens in one day, both negative and positive. If we do not take time to appreciate both, perhaps we will miss something that will help us grow. Our principles for living will guide us in recovery when we use them. We find it necessary to continue to do so on a daily basis.

Staying Clean on the Outside

Many of us first heard the Narcotics Anonymous message of recovery while in a hospital or institution of some kind. Transition from such places to the outside world is not easy under any circumstances. This is especially true when we are challenged with the changes which recovery brings. For many of us, early recovery was difficult. Facing the prospect of life without drugs can be very frightening. But those of us who made it through the early days found a life worth living. This pamphlet is offered as a message of hope to those now in a hospital or institution that you, too, can recover and live freely. Many of us have been where you are today. We have tried other ways, and many of us relapsed, some never to have another chance at recovery. We have written this pamphlet to share with you what we have found that works.

If you are able to go to meetings while you are in a hospital or institution, you can start developing good habits now. Come early and stay late at the meetings. Start, as soon as possible, to establish contacts with recovering addicts. If there are NA members from other groups attending your meetings, ask for their phone numbers and use them. Using these phone numbers will feel strange at first, even silly. But, given that isolation is at the core of the disease of addiction, that first phone call is a big stride forward. It isn't necessary to wait for a major problem to develop before calling someone in NA. Most members are more than willing to help in any way they can. This is also a good time to arrange for an NA member to meet you upon your release. If you already know some of the people you will be seeing at meetings when you are released, it will help you feel a part of the NA Fellowship. We cannot afford to be or feel alienated.

Staying clean on the outside means taking action. When you get out, go to a meeting the first day of your release. It is important to establish the habit of regular attendance. The confusion and excitement of "just getting out" has lulled some of us into thinking of taking a vacation from our responsibilities before settling down to the business of day-to-day living. This kind of rationalization has led many of us back to using. Addiction is a disease which takes no time off in its progression. If it is not arrested, it only becomes worse. What we do for our recovery today does not ensure our recovery tomorrow. It is a mistake to assume that the good intention of getting around to NA after a while will be sufficient. We must back up our intentions with action, the earlier the better.

If you will be living in a different town after your release, ask the NA members for a meeting list and the NA helpline number for your new area. They will be able to help you get in touch with NA groups and members where you will be living. You can also get information about meetings all over the world by writing to:

World Service Office
PO Box 9999
Van Nuys, CA 91409
USA

Sponsorship is a vital part of the NA program of recovery. It is one of the main channels through which newcomers can take advantage of the experience of NA members who are living the program. Sponsors can combine genuine concern for our well-being and a shared experience of addiction with solid knowledge of recovery in NA. We have found it works best to find a sponsor of your own sex. Choose a sponsor, even a temporary sponsor, as soon as possible. A sponsor helps you work through the Twelve Steps and Twelve Traditions of Narcotics Anonymous. A sponsor can also introduce you to other NA members, take you to meetings, and help you to get more comfortable in recovery. Our pamphlet, *Sponsorship*, contains additional information on the subject.

If we are to receive the benefits of the NA program, we must work the Twelve Steps. Along with regular meeting attendance, the steps are basic to our program of recovery from addiction. We have found that working the steps in order and continuously reworking them keeps us from relapsing into active addiction and the misery that it brings.

There is a variety of NA recovery literature available. The Little White Booklet and our Basic Text, *Narcotics Anonymous*, contain principles of recovery in our fellowship. Familiarize yourself with the program through our literature. Reading about recovery is a very important part of our program, especially when a meeting or another NA member might not be available. Many of us have found that reading NA literature on a daily basis has helped us maintain a positive attitude and has kept our focus on recovery.

When you begin going to meetings, get involved with the groups you attend. Emptying ashtrays, helping set up, making coffee, cleaning up after the meeting—all these tasks need to be done for the group to function. Let people know you are willing to help, and become a part of your group. Taking on such responsibilities is a necessary part of recovery and helps to counteract the feelings of alienation that can creep up on us. Such commitments, however small they may appear, may help ensure attendance at meetings when the *desire* to attend lags behind the *need* to attend.

It is never too early to establish a personal program of daily action. Taking daily action is our way of taking responsibility for our recovery. Instead of picking up that first drug, we do the following:

- Don't use, no matter what
- Go to an NA meeting
- Ask your Higher Power to keep you clean today
- Call your sponsor
- Read NA literature
- Talk to other recovering addicts

- Work the Twelve Steps of Narcotics Anonymous

We've discussed some of the things to do to stay clean; we should also discuss some things to avoid. In NA meetings, we often hear that we must change our old way of living. This means that we don't use drugs, no matter what! We have also found that we cannot afford to frequent bars and clubs or associate with people who use drugs. When we allow ourselves to hang around old acquaintances and places, we are setting ourselves up for relapse. When it comes to the disease of addiction, we are powerless. These people and these places never helped us stay clean before. It would be foolish to think things will be different now.

For an addict, there is no substitute for the fellowship of others actively engaged in recovery. It is important to give ourselves a break and give our recovery a chance. There are many new friends waiting for us in Narcotics Anonymous, and a new world of experiences lies ahead.

Some of us had to adjust our expectations of a completely different world once we were released. Narcotics Anonymous cannot miraculously change the world around us. It does offer us hope, freedom, and a way to live differently in the world by changing ourselves. We may find some situations which are no different than before, but, through the program of Narcotics Anonymous, we can change the way we respond to them. Changing ourselves does change our lives.

We want you to know that you are welcome in Narcotics Anonymous. NA has helped hundreds of thousands of addicts to live clean, to accept life on its own terms, and to develop a life that is truly worth living.

Recovery and Relapse

Many people think that recovery is simply a matter of not using drugs. They consider a relapse a sign of complete failure, and long periods of abstinence a sign of complete success. We in the recovery program of Narcotics Anonymous have found that this perception is too simplistic. After a member has had some involvement in our fellowship, a relapse may be the jarring experience that brings about a more rigorous application of the program. By the same token, we have observed some members who remain abstinent for long periods of time whose dishonesty and self-deceit still prevent them from enjoying complete recovery and acceptance within society. Complete and continuous abstinence, however, in close association and identification with others in NA groups, is still the best ground for growth.

Although all addicts are basically the same in kind, we do, as individuals, differ in degree of sickness and rate of recovery. There may be times when a relapse lays the groundwork for complete freedom. At other times that freedom can only be achieved by a grim and obstinate willfulness to hang on to abstinence, come hell or high water, until a crisis passes. An addict who by any means can lose, even for a time, the need or desire to use, and has free choice over impulsive thinking and compulsive action, has reached a turning point that may be the decisive factor in his recovery. The feeling of true independence and freedom hangs here, at times, in the balance. To step out alone and run our own lives again draws us, yet we seem to know that what we have has come from dependence on a Power greater than ourselves and from the giving and receiving of help from others in acts of empathy. Many times in our recovery the old bugaboos will haunt us. Life may again become meaningless, monotonous, and boring. We may tire mentally in repeating our new ideas and tire physically in our new activities, yet we know that if we fail to repeat them we will surely take up our old practices. We suspect that if we do not use what we have, we will lose what we have. These times are often the periods of our greatest growth. Our minds and bodies seem tired of it all, yet the dynamic forces of change or true conversion, deep within, may be working to give us the answers that alter our inner motivations and change our lives.

Recovery as experienced through our Twelve Steps is our goal, not mere physical abstinence. To improve ourselves takes effort, and since there is no way in the world to graft a new idea on a closed mind, an opening must be made somehow. Since we can do this only for ourselves, we need to recognize two of our seemingly inherent enemies, apathy and procrastination. Our resistance to change seems built in, and only a nuclear blast of some kind will bring about any alteration or initiate another course of action. A relapse, if we survive it, may provide the charge for the demolition process. A relapse and sometimes subsequent death of someone close to us can do the job of awakening us to the necessity for vigorous personal action.

Personal stories

Narcotics Anonymous has grown a great deal since 1953. The people who started this fellowship, for whom we have a deep and lasting affection, have taught us much about addiction and recovery. In the following pages, we offer you our beginnings. The first section was written in 1965 by one of our earliest members. More recent stories of NA members' recovery can be found in our Basic Text, Narcotics Anonymous.

We do recover

Although "Politics make strange bedfellows," as the old saying goes, addiction makes us one of a kind. Our personal stories may vary in individual pattern but, in the end, we all have the same thing in common. This common illness or disorder is addiction. We know well the two things that make up true addiction: obsession and compulsion. Obsession—that fixed idea that takes us back, time and time again, to our particular drug, or some substitute, to recapture the ease and comfort we once knew.

Compulsion—once having started the process with one fix, one pill, or one drink we cannot stop through our own power of will. Because of our physical sensitivity to drugs, we are completely in the grip of a destructive power greater than ourselves.

When, at the end of the road, we find that we can no longer function as human beings, either with or without drugs, we all face the same dilemma. What is there left to do? There seems to be this alternative: either go on as best we can to the bitter ends—jails, institutions, or death—or find a new way to live. In years gone by, very few addicts ever had this last choice. Those who are addicted today are more fortunate. For the first time in man's entire history, a simple way has been proving itself in the lives of many addicts. It is available to us all. This is a simple spiritual, not religious, program known as Narcotics Anonymous.

When my addiction brought me to the point of complete powerlessness, uselessness, and surrender some fifteen years ago,[2] there was no NA. I found AA, and in that fellowship met addicts who had also found that program to be the answer to their problem. However, we knew that many were still going down the road of disillusion, degradation, and death because they were unable to identify with the alcoholic in AA. Their identification was at the level of apparent symptoms and not at the deeper level of emotions or feelings, where empathy becomes a healing therapy for all addicted people. With several other addicts and some members of AA who had great faith in us and the program, we formed, in July of 1953, what we now know as Narcotics Anonymous.

[2] Written in 1965.

We felt that, now, the addict would find, from the start, as much identification as each needed to convince himself that he could stay clean by the example of others who had recovered for many years.

That this was what was principally needed has proved itself in these passing years. That wordless language of recognition, belief, and faith which we call empathy created the atmosphere in which we could feel time, touch reality, and recognize spiritual values long lost to many of us. In our program of recovery, we are growing in numbers and strength. Never before have so many clean addicts, of their own choice and in free society, been able to meet where they please, to maintain their recovery in complete creative freedom.

Even addicts said it could not be done the way we had it planned. We believed in openly scheduled meetings—no more hiding as other groups had tried. We believed this differed from all other methods tried before by those who advocated long withdrawal from society. We felt that the sooner the addict could face his problem in everyday living, just that much faster would he become a real, productive citizen. We eventually have to stand on our own feet and face life on its own terms, so why not from the start?

Because of this, of course, many relapsed, and many were lost completely. However, many stayed, and some came back after their setback. The brighter part is the fact that, of those who are now our members, many have long terms of complete abstinence and are better able to help the newcomer. Their attitude, based on the spiritual values of our steps and traditions, is the dynamic force that is bringing increase and unity to our program. Now, we know that the time has come when that tired old lie, "Once an addict, always an addict," will no longer be tolerated by either society or the addict himself. We do recover.

Telephone Numbers:

_____

_____

_____

_____

_____

_____

_____

_____

_____

_____

_____

_____

_____

_____

_____

_____